Tell Me About
Eternity

Published in Nashville, Tennessee, by Tommy Nelson®, a Division of Thomas Nelson, Inc.

Tommy Nelson® books may be purchased in bulk for educational, business, fund-raising, or sales promotional use. For information, please email SpecialMarkets@ThomasNelson.com.

Scripture quotations in this book are from the *International Children's Bible*®, *New Century Version*®, © 1986, 1988, 1999 by Tommy Nelson®, a Division of Thomas Nelson, Inc. All rights reserved.

Library of Congress Cataloging-in-Publication Data

Anderson, Joel.
  Tell me about eternity / by Joel Anderson ; illustrated by Joel Anderson
and Kristi Carter Smith.
      p. cm. — (Big topics for little kids)
  ISBN 1-4003-0598-5 (hardcover)
1. Eternity—Juvenile literature. 2. Future life—
Christianity—Juvenile literature. I. Smith, Kristi Carter. II. Title.
  BT910.A53 2005
  236'.21—dc22

                                        2005000005

Printed in China

05 06 07 08 09 RRD 5 4 3 2 1

big topics FOR little kids™

Tell Me About Eternity

by Joel Anderson

Illustrated by Joel Anderson
and Kristi Carter Smith

Tommy NELSON®

www.tommynelson.com
A Division of Thomas Nelson, Inc.
www.ThomasNelson.com

You made my whole being.
You formed me in my mother's body....
All the days planned for me
were written in your book
before I was one day old.

PSALM 139:13, 16

It was a very special day for two people.

One person was very young.

The other was very old.

Somehow they both knew this day was to be
one of the most important days of their lives.

They both had loving families around them.

They both could feel God's love like a warm hug.

They both were very helpless,
and they both were bald.

The young one wondered, *What will it be like out there?*
Should I be afraid? This is all I've ever known . . .
could I be happy anywhere else?

The older one wondered the same.

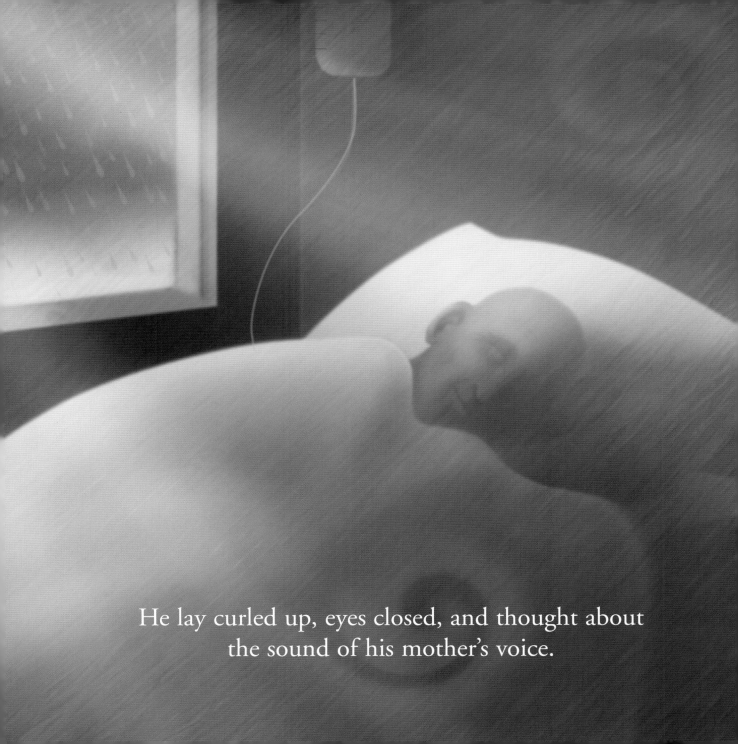

He lay curled up, eyes closed, and thought about the sound of his mother's voice.

The younger one did the same.

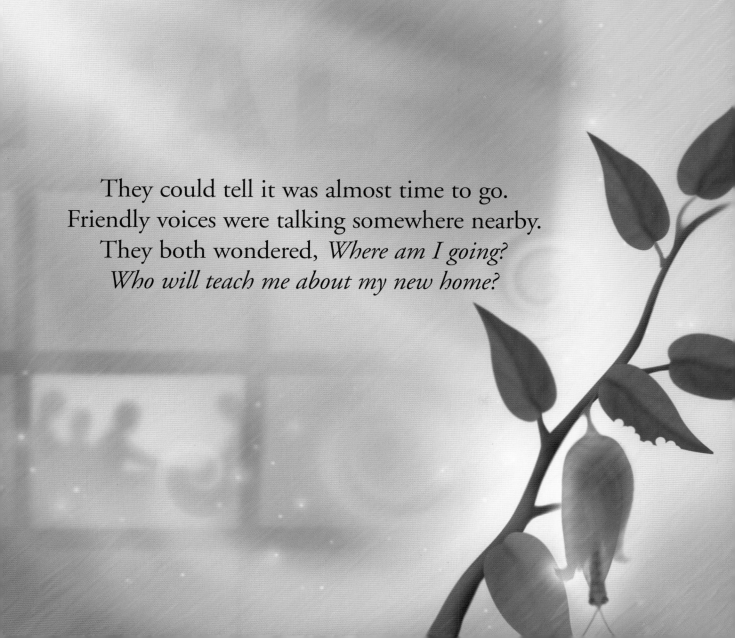

They could tell it was almost time to go.
Friendly voices were talking somewhere nearby.
They both wondered, *Where am I going?*
Who will teach me about my new home?

The young one felt herself
being pushed out of her quiet place.

The older one felt himself
being pulled toward heaven.

Both of them began to see bright and beautiful light.

They both could hear their names being called.

Into strong hands they were welcomed . . .

. . . Surrounded by loved ones laughing,
clapping, and singing for joy.

It was a wonderful time of celebration . . .

. . . on earth . . .

. . . and in heaven!

Dear friends,
now we are children of God.
We have not yet been shown
what we will be in the future.
But we know that when Christ
comes again, we will be like him.
We will see him as he really is.

1 JOHN 3:2

Parent / Teacher Discussion Aid

Q. How long is eternity?

A. Eternity is forever. It's hard to imagine because it has no beginning or end. God is eternal. He always has been and always will be.

Q. Were we created to live in eternity?

A. Yes! God made each of us in His image. That means each of us has a spirit that will live forever. Even though our earthly bodies will die, our spirits will keep on living for eternity. We will have wonderful new bodies that never get sick or tired. Our new bodies will never die again . . . they will be made to last forever!

Q. What will our new bodies be like?

A. After Jesus died and rose again, He was able to walk through walls, appear and disappear. He let His disciples touch His hands and side. He ate fish with them, too, so we know that He had a very different kind of new body! The Bible says this about our new bodies: "We know that our body—the tent we live in here on earth—will be destroyed. But when that happens, God will have a house for us to live in. It will not be a house made by men. It will be a home in heaven that will last forever" (2 Corinthians 5:1).

Q. Where were we before we were born?

A. The Bible says that before we were born, God knew us. All of the days of our lives were written in His book before we ever lived! God has no beginning or end. But each of us did have a beginning. When God started making us inside our mommies, we began a life that will never end. Each of us was born. Each of us lives for a while on the earth. Then each of us will keep on living forever in eternity.

Q. Where will we live in eternity?

A. The Bible says that God loved the world so much that He gave His only Son, so that whoever believes in Him should not perish, but have eternal life (John 3:16). Jesus said to trust in God, and trust in Him. Jesus said He is going to prepare a place for us, and will return to take us there (John 14:1–3). If you believe in Jesus, He has prepared a place for you in heaven where you will be with God for ever and ever!

Experiment for Little People

TOOLS

12 feet of string
1 marker

Draw a small dot (the size of the marker tip) near the beginning of the string. Roll out the rest of the string in a long line, or around the room.

The string is not eternal. It has a beginning and an end. But it will help you imagine eternity. If the string is eternity, then everything that has ever happened and everyone who has ever lived could fit inside the dot. So, even if our lives seem to last a long time, compared to eternity, they are actually very short!

Eternity lasts forever and ever! Jesus said that if you are His follower, He will go and prepare a place for you in heaven where you can be with Him for eternity!